Dance With Reflection

OrangeBooks Publication

1st Floor, Rajhans Arcade, Mall Road, Kohka, Bhilai, Chhattisgarh 490020

Website: **www.orangebooks.in**

© Copyright, 2024, Author

All rights reserved. No part of this book may be reproduced, stored in a retrieval system, or transmitted, in any form by any means, electronic, mechanical, magnetic, optical, chemical, manual, photocopying, recording or otherwise, without the prior written consent of its writer.

First Edition, 2024

DANCE
WITH REFLECTION

A RARE VIEW

KUMARI RASHMI

OrangeBooks Publication
www.orangebooks.in

This book is dedicated to all those who made me realize that Reflection in life is a necessity. Intuition is the driver, and life is reality. The book written by me is dedicated to my mother, who is self-explanatory. With the insight of My Nanaji, who is the best student of life, to my incessantly joyful Nani and others, I begin the journey of reflection.

Content

Preface 1

Part: 1

Reflection : A Rare View 4
[A life at present and Reflection at present] 4

Part: 2

Reflection : A Rear View 8
[A Rearview Shows What Is Past] 8

Part: 3

A Pause In Action 13
[The essence of pause in world of Motion] 13

Part: 4

Soulful Reflection 21
[Life For Bigger Cause] 21

Part: 5

Emotion Manifestation 31
[Different Emotions On Different Face] 31

Part: 6

Bird In Motion 41
[A Bird Express The Freedom] 41

Part: 7

Heart With Resolution 47
[Finding Greatness In Heart] 47

Part: 8

A Poem On Reflection 52
[Poetic Style] 52

Action And Reflection 55

Bibliography 56

HONEST DISCLOSURE 57

Quotes 58

Thank You Note 60

Preface

In no definite condition, life is lived. Dance with Reflection states the Life and Observation with Reality to Reflect.

Life cannot be chased; the need is to take a moment of pause. Reflection is now a rare view as it needs a presence in the present moment. Reflection on past is a rear view. It is a glimpse at not repeating erroneous past.

Maybe your expectations will be ruined, or your desperation will not be served.

A moment of Reflection is on the way.

Life does not need more information, but certainly, greatness in realization. The Heart is perfect to lead Reflection.

Dance with reflection brings you to your reflection. Every move is stillness at every gateway.

The glory cannot be your Guide, but Reflection is the best lamp to guide you at every junction. A life of dedication cannot be a life of Competition.

In dance with Reflection, the moves and dance are your own. You own music in action, as every reflection is a tribute to life and experiences. No amount of borrowing brings those sequential phases but in unplanned attire, as those were meant to lead to Greatness.

In those moments, where trading of essence was easy, holding moments of patience, perseverance, and truth, attire is always challenging. The Heart is a mirror for life. It owns every resolution of greatness, not grievances.

In each moment, the need is to be true to essence and nature. Dance with Reflection brings the moment of joy and tears. Living is the ultimate profoundness that serves Life.

Part: 1

Reflection : A Rare View

(A life at present and Reflection at present)

An inbound Activity; no invitation in reality. The presence of an observer is a necessity.

The arrival is here with the rarest view in Locality.

Reflection is a location within; a transformation within cannot be a computation. There cannot be delusion; when there is simplicity in action, there is Reflection. The indispensable part of Reality is the artful co-ordination to lead at Reflection.

The pure Heart and Soul have every light of satisfaction as it is a sacred destination.

WHEN HEART IS PERFECT,

WE JUST NEED REFLECTION.

It is impurities that count and Block the Ray of Reflection.

IF it is in a mirror, it is more than a facial expression.

IF it is in a heart, its need is of peaceful attention.

IF it is in the present moment, the need is for the present.

When you are inward,

No world to demonstrate, no pathways to hesitate.

A great way of living is not compensated with denomination. The present living cannot be negotiated with past perception.

The present to live and then to Reflect is "A Rare view". The Perception of present to live is that of Perception out of Fashion, and Present to Reflect with A pause is out of passion.

When hearts lead you, it is Darpan.

Your Mind does not own Darpan as you disown Samarpan.

The Pathways is of Reflection, with No Rules or restriction.

This happens when there is an arrival of REFLECTION.

Part: 2

Reflection : A Rear View
(A Rearview Shows What Is Past)

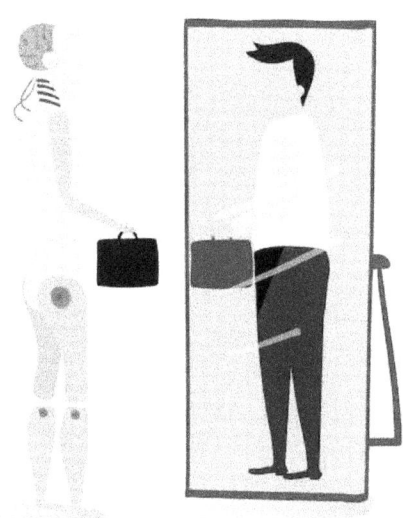

Rear views show the Past; Good or Bad becomes irrelevant. A Rear view is neither a place to live nor a place to drive out.

"Your past when compensates The Present.

The Life is compensated by an uncertain future."

The glimpse at the past gives an insight into present Reality, which is the essence of Reflection in the Past view.

A Rear view when becomes a Nostalgic city to Reside,

It is located in Bargain City.

Life at rear view is Reality when we forget the essence of Reality.

The Experiences of Life are incessant and different for each of us. How We live The Present with all those Experiences is a way to Reflect on Life and affection all around in places where we reside and visit. You cannot take one step forward and one step backward. This is dual living at a place of individuality.

When you reflect in rear view, you have Rear view to visit; A visit for Reflection.

When you depart, You cannot take every second glimpse of it.

THE REAR VIEW IS ALWAYS FOR RARE VIEW.

THE REAR VIEW IS ALWAYS FOR RARE VIEW.

THE PAST IS ALWAYS FOR PRESENT.

THE PAST IS ALWAYS FOR PRESENT.

THE PRESENT IS NOT FOR PAST.

THE PRESENT IS NOT FOR PAST.

The Reflection in the past is that part which is a necessity for every individual at every stage. The present is all that we own now, and we all have. A lens which Brings us closer to Reality. The Acceptance without compromises is The Acceptance without the dilution.

The Acceptance with the Dedication is all that brings necessity.

Life chooses to bring the brightest spot for Reflection. This is when you arrive at yourself. There is no entry to others; Exit to one that entered before yourself.

This cleans the Rear view, bringing the Rare.

It brings the present; it purifies us to live in Reality.

In simplest of expression, I say –

"Don't carry the baggage of the past when you are a host of the present".

The Reflection when becomes a part,

It is the essence of Art.

Part: 3

A Pause In Action
(The essence of pause in world of Motion)

Pause in motion is neither stoppage nor blockage.

A Pause in motion is the entrance to Gateway. A Gateway where there is a way for Reflection. A Gateway where there are movements towards Stillness.

Even alphabetically, In MOTION, "O" REPEATS TWO TIMES. So, Motion always has Repetition.

IN PAUSE, NO Alphabet repeats.

A Pause, whenever and wherever taken, is new finding and Reflection.

A pause in Action is a Reflection of intuition.

The Reflection arrives in the old fashion.

A pause in Motion takes you to the best Location. In the era of technology and information, inseparable elements are bustling. People run and slide into the Lap of Busyness. When all work in the same way, it is called Common and then generalized into concepts.

We are the ones who are born in the ages of races where Acknowledgement is for race. No one is looking at space and phases.

Welcome to the world of information.

These are popular when they should been at Rarity.

Whatever problem is in existential.

Whether it is of basics.

Whether it is of Demand or supply.

Whether it is of system.

Whether it is societally conditioned for belief.

The time arrives with Reflection as a beacon at an essential destination.

If it is the basics, which is wrong, we need to plant trees on barren land, but holding a water pot for a longer period is a necessity; a fertile one by planting trees and nurturing every day. We discover the basics as trees mature.

If it is of Demand or supply criteria, change market factors that affect Demand or Supply. All that affects need a change. The change of pathways where there is destruction or conundrum. Those who went in this way became invisible.

If it is a System, scrap the SYSTEM. The system is outdated.

When out of fashion is for clothes, which has no demand.

When you operate within Syllabus, A Question that covers wider aspects becomes out of the Syllabus.

It is time to change Human perception and Notions.

The greatest structural change is needed with a foundation combined with Devotion.

IF THIS IS NOT DONE, OUT OF LIVING WILL BE FOR HUMAN SPECIES.

If it is of Societal conditioned beliefs, Change the Terms or change the Definition. The change of Relevance to the change of Application will change the way how it is conditioned.

This will Liberate the Information. This will Liberate beliefs for Bigger Transformation.

The difference to adore. You may have different roles to associate with. You may have a different identity to resonate, but why live and be bounded by shorter boundaries? Live Life with Freedom.

You may be friends with someone: father, mother, son or many more.

You only have roles when you are you.

You first arrive at you, then at that pause, which will lead you to Reflection beyond you.

Life is quite short. How much you own is Unknown. The work follows at different places. The pause arrives to take you within The journey of Transformation.

The Great poet William Blake wrote in the book - The Marriage of Heaven and Hell,

"Energy is eternal delight, and he who desires, but acts not, breeds pestilence."

Yes, Energy is Delight; greatness arrives by the deep overflow of Energy That leads you to harmony within to flow. Energy is the source of everything from focus to consciousness. Energy leads to a higher purpose. When Man finds Joy in the presence of Nature, nature is the One that blesses us with the Element of all wisdom and great environment.

With A Pause with Reflection, there are ways to reach the point of greatest energy that overflows of energy at all spaces will give THE FREEDOM.

Every Pause gives different Insights, as the Pause is for greatness in the height.

A Pause without parameter.

A Pause without negotiation.

This is A Pause for Reflection.

This Pause in motion creates a Pathway for Soulful Reflection. When the present is lived, the joy is experienced; The arrival of rays for incessant joy creates that Reflection, which is of Reality and living at an inward destination and visiting to the outward destination.

Part: 4

Soulful Reflection
(Life For Bigger Cause)

The arrival at stillness creates a pathway to arrive at oneself and The Reality. Life is a blessing of innumerable potential. It is the pathways and discoveries that lead The Life beyond Information and The Life with Reflection.

Nature always deals with perfection. The Location of every Transformation is within reach. The arrival of oneself is a journey of self-knowledge to self-Reflection. In the outskirts of the present, there cannot be Reflection; it is the Present that can only hold soulful Reflection.

Welcome to the world beyond practicality,

where you go beyond the residence of individuality.

Bears the Indispensable Reality.

Life beyond Life expectancy.

The soulful Reflection is arrival at Spirituality.

The soulful Reflection is arrival at Liberation.

The arrival at Atman, The arrival at Siddhi.

The arrival at Truth, The Life: The Living is all to experience in Reality.

When one arrives, there is no dilemma to entertain or nothing to condition. The journey of arrival is of discovery within. The Meditation at every present. The meditation at every journey. When all stages are meditated on, it is travelled through Meditation.

When the Profoundness in Devotion is arrived, there is an arrival at a greater purpose. When He surrenders everything to the creator, He only owns the present.

The soulful Reflection is Rotation at the axis of Life. When living is found within, The Reflection is found at the axis of Life. The sphere of Life is of automation. A complete dynamic path remains untold that creates a path for Soulful Reflection.

When Life holds its axis, whoever awaits with a question eventually finds the answer. The Reflection is automated at every pathway. Travel is experienced through actions that lead to reflection. Every pathway that creates its own way is a blissful one to travel and blessed to be part of the journey.

Reflection on life's blessing is the way that leads to the Truth, which is the best part of life. When the essence of Acceptance leads to

Reflection at every junction, there is the existence of satisfaction.

In the world of calculation, the arrival at a higher purpose is of arrival without calculation. This is the space beyond information that will lead to Transformation. There is no demand for preconceived notions and no notorious celebration when leading to Soulful Reflection.

In the world of dual space, when ownership of Authenticity creates liability, this world will close every door of entrance which is of Non-Duality. The realm of locality of sincerity, Authenticity and immense satisfaction is Soulful Reflection.

This world will limit your intention.

When intention is limited, there is half location.

This world will limit intuition.

When intuition is limited, there is a dual location.

This world will limit Action.

When Action is limited, there is no location.

A Dilemma is anxiousness at the gateway of motion. What to do is not known for perfection. What not to do is lose connection. In desperate emotion, the half-lived is reality, as neither boredom is lived nor happiness is cherished.

That instant plate serves all dishes of complication. It brought the pleasure of masquerade beauty perceived as reality. That two-minute gain served lifelong pain. There is nothing to blame for the blockage.

The lost Equanimity could not be traced because no one was on the way to search operations in any space. The entertainment becomes the entertainer, the viewer becomes the other entertainer. A different purpose was implemented at a similar station.

This leads to complication and competition but no relevance to Reflection. A soulful Reflection could not be found because there was lost intuition.

In a no-comparison world, there is soulful Reflection. It is the divine space of purity and is connected to nature's beauty. The nature with the essence of perfection in creation in that view at the reflection site, where there is an open heart without condition.

THIS REFLECTION IS NOT RELATED TO MIRROR ONLY. THIS REFLECTION IS RELATED TO LIFE AND INTUITION.

THE ONE WITHOUT DEFINITION IS THE ONE THAT IS SOULFUL REFLECTION.

A Blank Sheet For Reflection

A Blank sheet for your Reflection

Part: 5

Emotion Manifestation
[Different Emotions On Different Face]

In the era of display of emotions, there remain half revelations at Emotion manifestation. What is told is half hidden backwards; what remains untold is unknown at every destination. The Emotion Manifestation is an untold story.

Emotion is a display of action in motion. Some are inward in the rotation phase, some outwards in Reflection. It is a complete set of silenced Perfection: Happiness to Sadness, Anxiety to Hatred, Horrified to Cheated, Hopeful to amused, and Exuberance to Frustration. When all is combined, it results in Emotion, and when displayed in Reflection, it is Emotion manifestation.

There is greatness all around that some reside and some besides without being aware. When unaware, Greatness is sidelined without manifestation. Those beliefs are of half as full, cost every greatness. The life when transacted with the Emotion, the Deal was of success in monetary transaction but failed at Emotions.

The emotions were borrowed without any obligation. The life of an emotion card is issued with validity at every location. This will be called a new invention. A card of emotion swiped for emotionless connection. A human arrives without emotions.

This is half of the emotion lived in the present; the other half believed in the past and future. There cannot be a complete one to live when half exists in belief. There is a Diversion from genuine emotion as loss is cherished with celebration.

The forefront and behind are equally important in this case. When you hide behind feelings, you make common sense served on a common plate. When you reside behind, you become a pretender rather than actually feeling the emotion.

In the age of technologically driven information, Artificial intelligence is driving humans to outdated manifestations by the display of falsified diversion. A race of comparison, competition and confiscation of the impeccable potential. When a Human is capped, it means he is trapped. Emotions of different colors are displayed at the gateway of emotion.

HAPPINESS is the emotion of rarity. Happiness arrives only at a close gateway of few desires. It is the stillness of other emotions with

Serendipity in actions. Happiness is a beautiful emotion of perfection. It is realizing the one that cannot be taught and explained in words of alphabets and numeric datasets. The emotion of greatness in the present is happiness, and it is without definition.

A feeling of SADNESS drives every Reflection at forefront. Sadness is a feeling of unhappiness or sorrow with clear cause and unclear flaws. The inevitable phase with adversities with clear faces drives sadness at all stages. When life changes, it leads you to sadness in phases.

ANXIETY: A feeling of future adverse anticipation with a sense of uncertainty that deviates from reality. There is an adverse implication in the present. Different type of anxiety exists, but most of them are driven by fear and mind games. Anxiety always loses the Present.

ANGER is a difficult one to explain. Anger is cherished Lollipop of the generation and the most debated emotion. A difficult one to comprehend, as there are different dimensions. It is sometimes driven by expectations.

This is the best quote on this emotion.

This is an abstract from the book- Auto-biography of a yogi, by Paramhansa Yogananda.

"Wrath springs only from thwarted desires. I do not expect anything from others, so their actions cannot be in opposition to wishes of mine."

The way I understand it: Wrath is Anger. Anger is caused by want or desire that was not met. Every

Expectation creates a loop of another expectation that drives emotions. I hold a clean mind to your actions, and I am not a broadcaster of unsatisfied emotion regarding your actions.

The Anger is that wing that paved the path for Every Dissatisfaction. Every drop of energy is wasted with Expectation of another location, which results in anger in action.

When a complication is cherished with Duality,

Life is lived without Sincerity.

A Man has man faces of revelation in wide areas of life phases. He has roles to play and bills to pay in the lifespan. He is trapped in his own ideas and lacked an understanding of the basics. When sponsored by emotion, he reveals 'The Unexpectation'.

A person's face is of wider relevance. If you look at his life from childhood to old age, you will be accountable for improper emotions. In Multicity of Emotions, He does not know his real one. In Pretension, he loses his real retentions.

When the loss was cherished with popularity on a plate of fame, the result was a broken reality. He pretended to be nice in public spaces; he was miserable in private phases. The public faces to roam, private ones without drones, a different face according to affordability and many more covered ones with complexity.

When He is communicating with himself, He owns the hidden faces. He now resides behind a hidden reflection. This one with a lot of emotions, and there is an Emotional Manifestation. When his faces have no attire, He inbounds with Reflection.

The significance of authentic Emotion is rare as the rise of transacted emotion is in the locality. Every game for half fame is now the biggest adversity. An outsourced one is the implementation with popularity.

The need is Reflection at the gateway of Emotion. The Reflection will bring to Originality with Emotional Manifestation. The power of Manifestation is greatness to reside. The manifestation power is of that greatest possibility of infinity, which is of consciousness and Realization.

In the realm of every possibility, the driver is The Manifestation. The Reflections recalls everything said in the world of connection. The Visualization of manifestation is greatness in action.

With all the Complexity and confusion, the significance of Emotional Manifestation is the path to simplification. The path of patience, perseverance and the present can only be lived with the essence of Life.

Part: 6

Bird In Motion

[A Bird Express The Freedom]

Birds are beautiful creation; they are nature's reflection,

Bird in motion is a beautiful expression of freedom.

The flying of birds is that beautiful journey of Freedom that has infinity to touch in motion. The bird governs that state of freedom that is inexplicable. The receptor of uniqueness is not bounded by definition; this is why the birds are perfect creations.

The birds fly with a special ability of Aerodynamics; Aerodynamics is simply how objects move around Air.

The combination of the physical forces of lift, drag, weight and thrust helps the bird fly. The bird flies using its wings. Birds fly through the flapping motion of their wings up and down. As a bird flaps its wings, it creates an upward force called Lift.

The bird flies in motion with takeoff from a stationary position and ends with landing. When a bird lands, it gradually reduces its speed and altitude. The slowness is greatness in motion.

These are beautiful emotions,

This is a perfect motion of observation.

Small birds, when first fly, express the essence of Nature. When they first fly, they express a taste of freedom. These birds generally fly at sunset time. The observation of small birds provides a glimpse of all existence. It expresses how small and pure efforts drive everything.

The innocence with which they play is beautiful joy at sight.

The birds enjoy flying with basic learning.

When Air resistance is high, they achieve greatness in motion and emotion.

These birds have great and beautiful communication.

They have an intuitive conversation.

The bird, when forced to live in cramped cages, shows human belief in the condition. Humans lived with deceitful notions when they were caged. "Freedom".

The Bird's contribution to Nature is immense from the medium of Communication to harmony in nature. The Rarity of birds chirping in the morning in the township is a Reflection of the environment where birds do not like places where they do not have trees to reside and hide.

IF BIRD WROTE TO HUMANITY, THEY WILL PROBABLY WRITE-

"In the world of filters and purifiers,

You are replacing the original with artificial.

A water purifier for water is Good.

BUT

For thought impure.

Living conditioned.

These impurities cannot be filtered; there is no manufactured filtration.

You failed by your own description."

A relevant and genuine revelation by birds to humans.

FREEDOM IS NOT A CAGE OF DEFINITION

NEITHER BOUND BY CONDITION

BIRDS ARE PHILOSOPHER IN MOTION.

The philosophy station is ready. The birds in motion arrive at philosophy station.

With the pause, the birds have yet to arrive; with motion and Reflection they arrive.

Great living is never the condition that is asked but lived for but not in return with tradeoff analysis. Birds in action never bear half the permission of the cage. They arrive with the truth to fly.

Part: 7

Heart With Resolution
(Finding Greatness In Heart)

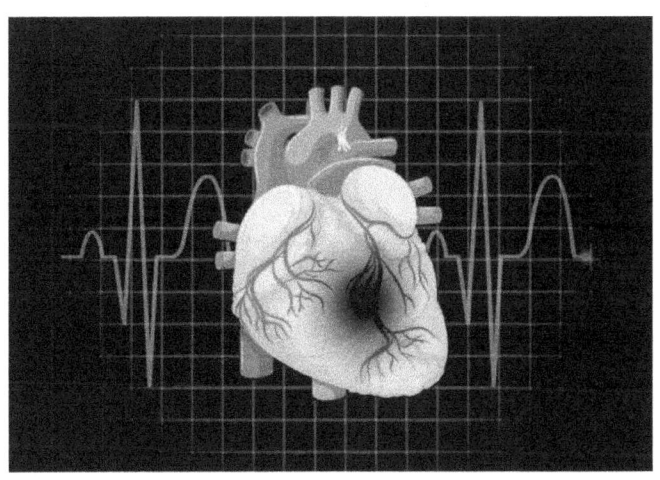

The Heart is the hub of all sacred places. The heart is a dwelling space of self. Among all the places to visit, the Journey of the heart is the most stunning.

The voice of Heart and the voice of Mind are difficult to differentiate. The need is to be closer to life and then the voice of the heart will be audible. The voice of the heart will bring you to your true nature. It will bring harmony around.

The voice of mind brings,

Past to cheer, Future to fear.

But the Present is always lost.

In attire of Ego, the voice of the mind echoes.

In arrogance, voice of mind mislead you.

In rationality, it searches for a reason to trap you.

When the voice of mind is the voice of smartness and balanced in structure.

The voice of the heart is pure. It brings truth along its way. Neither dramatizing nor alluring, Just bringing sincerity along with actions and silence. It will never walk on the path of belonging. As you travel, the leeway along the ways will rise above belief and social condition.

Heart sings a tune of Raindrop.

Heart holds the ground of flow.

Heart holds a mirror of affection.

This is the beauty of the heart and the heart space.

THE BEAUTIFUL EXPRESSION OF HEART IN TERMS OF HEART I HAVE FOUND IS FROM CHANDOGYA UPANISHAD.

Verse 8.1.3

"यावान्वा अयमाकाशस्तावानेषोऽन्तर्हृदय अकाश उभे अस्मिन्द्यावापृथिवी अन्तरेव समाहिते उभावग्निश्च वायुश्च सूर्याचन्द्रमसावुभौ विद्युन्नक्षत्राणि यच्चास्येहास्ति यच्च नास्ति सर्वं तदस्मिन्समाहितमिति" |

Meaning –

[The teacher replies:]

'The space in the heart is as big as space outside. Heaven and Earth are both within it, and so are fire and air, the sun and the moon, lightning and the stars. Everything exists within that space in the embodied self, whatever it has or does not have.'

My understanding: The heart is not about the measurement of length or breadth of spaces. The place where everything is grounded. The heart is the place where the soul resides. The boundless, the timeless is related to the heart. The heart is an existential part of creation. It Contains the totality of nature. The Heart is the best locality.

In the world of paucity of affection, the need is to be a Citizen of Heart. As it has nature, Reflection and affection incessantly. The non-dual world is the world of the heart. The never-ending space is the Heart space.

When heart is beautiful in motion.

The heart is beautiful with stillness.

Part: 8

A Poem On Reflection
(Poetic Style)

Dance With Reflection

In the darkness of banalities,

In a moment of complexity,

The presence of reflection is a necessity.

It serves as the best creativity.

What do you bring when nothing exists on the table?

What you see when you are surrounded by duality.

The act of revered action,

The act of surrendered devotion.

This creates a moment of reflection.

This creates a moment of reflection.

It becomes a moment of realization.

It becomes a life station.

Reflection without equation.

It is a soulful connection.

At that observer station,

Reflection arrives at Life Location.

When close to truth is only action,

All transactions are non-essential notions.

That's the beauty of Reflection.

That's the beauty of Reflection.

Action And Reflection

In the sincerest approach, I request you to plant a tree that grows with the Journey of Reflection. This will bring you closer to nature and observation into life.

The stillness into life.

The growth takes time.

The undeniable nature and its role, and many other lessons will be taught by trees in a practical way.

Bibliography

The Great poet William Blake's book- The Marriage of Heaven and Hell.

An abstract from the book - Autobiography of a Yogi by Paramhansa Yogananda.

Satish Dhawan – Bird Flight.

Raman memorial lecture, 1988.

A Verse from Chandogya Upanishad

HONEST DISCLOSURE

As a reader and writer, I understand that books have the space to give you new insight. From theoretical ground to practical ground, Books lead you to the pathway of Reflection. The ability to lead pathways is about practicality and action. Books are a superpower for all. I don't falsify any hope that this will drastically change something. In the Reflective sphere, I wish you to find life and essence.

Quotes

Written by Kumari Rashmi

"We are equal in an Unequal way."

"Modernization is about not losing essence."

"Freedom is the most beautiful association. One who lives cannot cage others in pursuit of decoration."

"When falsity is the host, genuineness is lost."

"You are a combination of action you do and stories you combine."

"What works for you is your treasurer."

"TIME, TRUTH AND PRESENT cannot be negotiated."

Thank You Note

With the journey along, I thank you for considering it worthwhile. The simplest thing is the most beautiful and valuable. In a Journey of Reflection, you connect to life. In that sphere of resources, I hope I added some insight into the journey of reading. Thank you for deciding this one to read.

Namaste

Author Location

For writing engagement and private Discourse with sincerity, With Open heart, and devotion the author is available at:

Twitter @rashmi_kr2

YouTube Channel:

1. PROFOUND DEVOTION

2. Writer@PE

LinkedIn:

https://www.linkedin.com/in/kumari-rashmi

-b4401b248

Medium = *medium.com/@krashmi*

GMail =*krirashmi760@gmail.com*